WARRIORS & WEAPONS

DUNGEONS & DRAGONS®

WARRIORS & WEAPONS

A Young Adventurer's Guide

WRITTEN BY JIM ZUB

WITH STACY KING AND ANDREW WHEELER

TEN SPEED PRESS
California | New York

CONTENTS

INTRODUCTION

This is a fantasy story.

You are the main character.

Who are you?

What do you do?

This book is a way to answer those two very important questions. It's a guide to the fascinating races that populate the world of DUNGEONS & DRAGONS and the combat-centered classes that define their role as adventurers. It gives you a wide range of options to choose from, along with armor, weapons, and other equipment to outfit your heroic persona.

Read this book from start to finish, or open it to any spot, get pulled in by the exciting illustrations, and start brainstorming from there. The more you read, the more character ideas will spring from your imagination.

Every character is unique. Even when two of them share the same race and class, the decisions they make will take them on an exclusive journey that is yours to tell. DUNGEONS & DRAGONS is all about building memorable characters, and the legends of your grand deeds are about to begin.

Have fun!

HUMAN **DWARF** **ELF** **GNOME**

HALF-ELF **HALF-ORC** **HALFLING** **DRAGONBORN**

KENKU **TABAXI** **TIEFLING** **TORTLE**

FANTASY RACES

Creating a new character involves understanding the traits they share with you and the traits they don't. Part of that comes from inside, their attitudes and personalities, but other parts are outward and physical because in this wondrous world of fantasy, you can be something other than human. By choosing a character's race, you gain a unique appearance and interesting abilities. Each of the twelve options presented here are filled with potential that you can unlock when you decide to make one of them yours and start to build your character's story.

HUMAN

DO YOU LONG TO MAKE YOUR MARK ON THE WORLD?

DO YOU LIVE IN THE MOMENT YET PLAN FOR THE FUTURE?

ARE YOU BRAVE AND AMBITIOUS?

YOU, YES YOU, MIGHT BE A HUMAN!

AGE Humans reach adulthood after about two decades and generally live less than a century.

SIZE Adult humans vary wildly in height and build, but most stand between five feet and just over six feet tall and weigh between 100 and 250 pounds.

Humans are the youngest of the common races, late to appear in the world and short-lived compared to dwarves (see page 6), elves (see page 8), and halflings (see page 16). Ambitious and far-reaching, humans make the most of their short lives, whether by exploration, innovation, or the founding of great empires. They are the most adaptable of all the races, and can be found in the remote corners of the world, from vast deserts and tropical islands to mighty mountains and snow-swept plains.

Diversity is a hallmark of the human species. There is no typical appearance—they may be pale to dark skinned, tall or short, with hair that crosses the spectrum of both shade and texture. Their customs, morals, and tastes vary, too. Where they settle, they stay—building cities and kingdoms that persist long after their mortal lifespans have ended. Unlike other races, human communities tend to be welcoming of outsiders as mingling places for all.

Humans who seek adventure are the most daring and ambitious members of a daring and ambitious race. Many are driven by the desire for glory, adventuring to amass power, wealth, and fame. Others are inspired by personal causes, such as a desire to protect their home from danger, to seek out hidden knowledge, or to satisfy their curiosity about the world.

VARIETY IS THE SPICE OF LIFE
Humans come from the most varied backgrounds of all characters, giving them access to more knowledge, more languages, and more homeland choices than the other fantasy races.

ATTRIBUTES

Adaptable Humans' flexible nature means that they can easily learn new skills and abilities, giving them an edge when studying or training.

DWARF

DO YOU VALUE HARD WORK AND FAMILY?

DO YOU SOMETIMES HOLD A GRUDGE?

ARE YOU ALWAYS ON THE LOOKOUT FOR TREASURE?

YOU MIGHT BE A DWARF!

AGE Dwarves are recognized as adults by age twenty, but are still considered "young" until age fifty. They live to an average age of 350 years.

SIZE Adult dwarves stand four to five feet tall and weigh around 150 pounds.

S tout and endlessly loyal, dwarves are a people who value tradition and the bonds of clan and family. They are short but strong as well as resilient due to a harsh life on the mountains, making them quite adept for their demanding work as miners.

Dwarven culture is built around mining. Its rewards inform why dwarves have such a powerful appreciation for the splendor of gold and jewels (and the value of solid iron weapons), and its challenges explain why they form such tight-knit communities that are often hostile to possible rivals, most notably goblins and orcs.

Dwarves can be stubborn and single-minded, which means feuds between rival clans can last for generations. Dwarves that bring their crafting skills to cities far from home will never forget where they come from. In fact, honoring a clan tradition or avenging an ancient wrong are common reasons for dwarves to head out on adventures, though they might also go exploring for the sake of personal glory, in service to one of their industrious gods, or simply for the chance to get more gold!

DWARVEN FEUDS Dwarves have a strong sense of justice and deep loyalty to their clan traditions. A wrong done to one dwarf is considered a slight against the entire clan, which means one insult, if not apologized for quickly enough, can become a full-blown clan feud lasting for generations.

ATTRIBUTES

Tough Physically robust, dwarves can take a lot of hits, and they have a natural resistance to poison.

Handy Dwarves love to develop their expertise in certain crafts, whether it's forging weapons or cutting stone. They know the tools of their trade inside out.

Strong Dwarves that live in tough terrain, like cold and rugged mountains, are particularly noted for their physical strength.

Wise Dwarves that live in less hostile terrain tend to be highly perceptive. Away from the shelter of their mines, they've learned to keep their wits about them.

ELF

DO YOU LOVE MAGIC AND
ARCANE MYSTERIES?

DO YOU FEEL OLDER AND
WISER THAN YOUR YEARS?

DO YOU PREFER DIPLOMACY
RATHER THAN PHYSICAL
CONFRONTATION?

YOU MIGHT BE An ELF!

SIZE Elves are generally a bit shorter than humans. They are typically very slender and beautiful!

AGE Elves mature at about the same rate as humans but consider themselves childlike and inexperienced until about their 100th birthday. They typically live for more than 700 years.

There are places in the world that don't quite seem real; areas of breathtaking beauty where the magic of other realms spills through into our own. It's in these locations that you're most likely to encounter elves, a race known for their elegance, grace, and gifts of enchantment.

Born of otherworldly magic, elves live for centuries, and often seem unfazed by the presence and actions of more short-lived creatures. They prefer to remain in their own secluded communities, but may venture out to share their artistic gifts or martial skills with the world, or to expand their understanding of other cultures. Elves cherish diplomacy and avoid violence if they can, preferring to rely on civility and cunning to resolve conflicts. An elf might master swordplay without ever engaging in actual battle!

Elven society generally falls into three categories. High elves are the most refined, the most haughty, and the most devoted to magic. Wood elves are in touch with the natural world and the skills needed to survive in the wild. Dark elves, also called drow, have adapted to life underground. Though they have a reputation for wickedness, one must never be too quick to judge. After all, being predictable is boring, and elves hate to be boring.

FAVORED WEAPONS Elves excel at armed combat and specialize in different weapons, such as longswords, longbows, crossbows, and rapiers.

ATTRIBUTES

Grace Elves are as dexterous in combat as they are in dance.

Magic Naturally gifted in magic, many elves can perform some simple spells without any study, and all elves have a high resistance to enchantment.

Vigilance Elves have refined senses. They can see clearly in the dark and are very alert to strange sights and sounds. Elves do not need sleep, which makes them excellent at performing watch duties!

GNOME

ARE YOU FASCINATED BY
HOW THE WORLD WORKS?

DO YOU SOMETIMES TALK
TOO MUCH?

DO YOU LONG TO SEE THE
WORLD AND MAKE NEW
FRIENDS ALONG THE WAY?

YOU MIGHT BE A GNOME!

SIZE Adult gnomes stand just over three feet tall, about half the height of a tall human. They weigh about 45 pounds.

AGE Gnomes reach adulthood by about age twenty and live for 350 to 500 years.

The small bodies of gnomes hold big personalities, filled with humor, happiness, and positivity that shine forth from their smiling faces. They live in bustling communities carved out of hillsides, where the sounds of hard work and laughter fill the air, though many of them will travel far and wide to seek out adventure and get as much excitement out of life as they can. They always see the best in other people and will often be enthusiastic to join an adventuring party, though their talkativeness can be exhausting for some. They have a lot to say and are happy to share it all!

Gnomes' love of learning makes itself known in their passion for taking on hobbies—and because they live long lives, they can hone their skills in fine crafts, such as woodworking, engineering, inventing, or the study of magic and alchemy. Gnomes never worry about making mistakes, because every error is another opportunity to learn and grow. If there is a bright side to any situation, or a positive way to look at any encounter, a gnome will find it.

GNOMISH NAMES Gnomes love names, and most have a half-dozen or so! These range from the formal, three-part names they use around non-gnomes to affectionate nicknames bestowed by family and friends. Gnomes favor names that are fun to say, such as Zook, Boddynock, Ellyjobell, or Stumbleduck.

ATTRIBUTES

Intellect Gnomes are known for their wit, charm, and smarts, and will often try to talk their way out of difficult situations.

Industrious Many gnomes are natural tinkerers who build wonderful clockwork toys and devices.

Dexterity Gnomes have strong reflexes and an excellent sense of balance. They might prefer to duck out of a fight rather than fight back.

Tricky Many gnomes have a gift for stealth and illusion, allowing them to mask their presence or easily slip away from trouble.

HALF-ELF

HALF-ELF NAMES Half-elves raised among humans are often given elvish names, and vice versa.

AGE Half-elves mature much like humans, reaching adulthood in their early twenties, but live much longer—often more than 180 years!

SIZE Half-elves are about the same size as humans, ranging from five to six feet tall and weighing between 100 and 180 pounds.

Born between two worlds but belonging to neither, half-elves are conceived in rare romances between mortal humans and mystic elves. As such, they combine the best qualities of both: human curiosity and ambition softened by the refined senses and artistry of the elves.

Half-elves are also destined to live apart from society. Among elves, they become grown adults while their peers remain children; among humans, they watch friends and family age while they themselves carry on seemingly untouched by time. Many choose solitary lives as a result, although others take advantage of their natural charm and grace to find a place at the heart of their communities, serving as leaders and diplomats. Their long lives often lead to wandering, drawing them into an adventurer's existence among other misfits who understand their outsider status.

Half-elves appear elvish to humans and human to elves. Their features may be a perfect blend of both parents, or favor one side of their heritage over the other. Their eyes are usually elven, large and luminous in shades of gold or silver. Half-elf men may grow facial hair, and some adopt a beard to conceal their elven lineage. Their chaotic spirits value personal freedom above all, and they fare poorly when bound by too many rules or expectations.

ATTRIBUTES

Darkvision Elven heritage has gifted half-elves with superior vision in dark and low-light conditions.

Fey Ancestry The magic of their fairy ancestors makes half-elves immune to sleep spells. They are also difficult to charm by magical means.

Charisma Half-elves combine the grace of elves with the appeal of humans, making it easy for them to find friends wherever they go!

Chaotic Spirit Like their elven forebears, half-elves are drawn to chaos. They find creative solutions to problems but can be unpredictable at times!

HALF-ORC

DO YOU HAVE STRONG EMOTIONS—BOTH JOY AND RAGE?

ARE YOU DETERMINED AND STUBBORN?

DO YOU VALUE ACTION OVER CONTEMPLATION?

YOU MIGHT BE A **HALF-ORC**!

AGE Half-orcs mature faster than humans and are considered adults after 14 years. They continue to age more rapidly throughout their lives, rarely surviving more than 75 years.

SCARS Among orcs, scars are an important mark of status. Battle scars denote victory, while other wounds serve as badges of shame or punishment. Any half-orc who has lived among orcs will bear such scars, whether good or bad. Some hide these marks when among non-orcs, while others flaunt their scars to intimidate enemies or honor their heritage.

SIZE Half-orcs are larger and bulkier than humans. They range from six to seven feet tall and weigh between 180 and 250 pounds.

Where human and orc communities have learned to live in harmony, half-orcs may be found. Even when raised by humans, there is no hiding their heritage: their grayish skin, sloping foreheads, prominent teeth, and towering builds make it clear that they have orcish blood. Half-orcs most often live within orc communities, although some may be raised within human settlements.

The rage felt by all orcs runs through half-orc veins, burning like fire. Half-orcs feel all their emotions deeply, whether blinding fury or boisterous glee. Insults deeply strike their pride, and sadness saps their strength. Physical pleasures—such as feasting, wrestling, and wild dancing—bring them great joy. They are often short-tempered and sullen, and it takes little for an argument to escalate into a fight.

Half-orcs struggle to find acceptance wherever they go. Many races, including humans, distrust them, while fellow orcs may taunt or bully them because of their perceived diminutive size. While some half-orcs are content to survive solely on brute strength, others are driven to prove their worth to the wider world. With their physical prowess and relentless nature, half-orcs make fearsome adventurers, renowned for their mighty deeds and notorious for their savage fury.

ATTRIBUTES

Relentless Endurance When badly injured, half-orcs can call upon great reserves of strength and energy to avoid unconsciousness, staying on their feet to continue the battle.

Savage Attacks When they make a critical hit, half-orcs can add their innate brute strength to the blow, increasing the damage significantly.

Menace Their size and rough appearance makes it easy for half-orcs to intimidate others! They can often bluff their way out of a fight—although most prefer to let their fists swing.

Darkvision Their orcish heritage gives half-orcs superior vision in dark and low-light conditions.

HALFLING

DO YOU SEE THE GOOD
IN EVERYONE?

DO YOU VALUE FAMILY AND
FRIENDS OVER FAME
AND FORTUNE?

ARE YOU BRAVE ENOUGH TO
FACE DANGERS MANY TIMES
YOUR SIZE?

YOU MIGHT BE A HALFLING!

SIZE Adult halflings stand about three feet tall and weigh 40 to 45 pounds.

AGE Halflings are considered adults by age twenty and can live up to 150 years.

Halflings are friendly, cheerful people inspired by the values of family, home, and simple pleasures. Short and stout, they like to wear bright colors that contrast with their ruddy skin, brown to hazel eyes, and brown hair. Most live in small, peaceful communities within the kingdoms of other races. Displays of wealth and status don't impress them, and there is no halfling royalty. Instead they are ruled by the wisdom of their elders, although there is always room for capable young halflings to make a name for themselves.

Halflings are a curious people, interested in even the most ordinary details about the world. This curiosity, rather than a love of gold or glory, is the inspiration for most young halflings who become adventurers. Others are driven by a danger to their community, putting themselves at risk to protect their families and their friends. Halflings excel at finding simple, practical solutions to problems and bring a touch of home comforts wherever they go. Many an adventuring party has been grateful for the warmth and good cheer that a halfling companion can create in even the most desolate of dungeons!

THE UNSEEN HALFLING

Their small size and innate stealth help halflings excel at avoiding unwanted attention. They can slip through busy crowds without being noticed, giving them a great advantage when gathering information or sneaking away from a fight!

ATTRIBUTES

Luck Their knack for finding practical solutions can sometimes give halflings a second chance to correct their mistakes.

Bravery Stout of heart as well as of body, halflings will face dangers that cause other adventurers to flee.

Nimbleness Because they are so small, halflings can evade the attacks of larger creatures!

Stealth Their short stature makes it easy for halflings to hide and avoid unwanted attention.

DRAGONBORN

AGE Dragonborn mature quickly, reaching full adulthood by the age of 15 years. They live to around 80 years old. Dragonborn commonly have one simple name in childhood and take on a different moniker to mark their transition into adulthood.

DRAGONBORN COLORS Most dragonborn scales are brass or bronze in tone. Red, rust, copper-green, and gold hues are also common. A few clans still have a strong bloodline connection to their founding dragon and, in these rare cases, brighter colors, including blue, green, and shining white, can be found.

SIZE Dragonborn are usually taller than most humans, and much more heavily built, with thick hides that make them heavier still. They lack the wings and tails of their dragon relatives, however.

Dragons are some of the most powerful and terrifying creatures you might ever meet. Their humanoid kin, the dragonborn, are a lot more approachable, but still kind of scary!

Descended from dragons and shaped by draconic magic, dragonborn are a noble warrior race, with dragonlike features and powers inherited from their ancestors. These skills are tied to specific types of destructive energy, which are often reflected in the color of the dragonborn's scaly hide. They live in clans that are often linked to a specific class of dragon ancestor, and they proudly worship their dragon gods. Clans are the heart of dragonborn society, and all dragonborn know their duty and strive to serve to their best abilities, whether that means being a great warrior, a great craftsperson, or a great cook. Failure brings shame to the clan, and excellence brings honor. As descendants of arguably the most noble and mighty of all creatures, they feel they have a lot to live up to.

Dragonborn will rarely look beyond their clans for assistance, yet they find that sometimes the best way to serve their clan and honor their gods is to leave everything behind and set out on an adventure, pursuing a great quest or bringing glory to their people.

ATTRIBUTES

Strength Draconic heritage imbues all dragonborn with great physical power.

Breath Weapon Dragonborn can exhale the type of destructive energy associated with their ancestry! Some dragonborn breathe fire, but others expel bolts of lightning, bursts of cold, streams of acid, or clouds of poison.

Resistance Dragonborn have a natural resistance to whatever destructive energy they possess, so a dragonborn who breathes fire is immune to fire, and a dragonborn who breathes acid is invulnerable to acid.

KENKU

AGE A short-lived species, kenku reach maturity at 12 years old and can live up to 60 years.

AN ANCIENT CURSE The kenku once served a powerful entity on another plane of existence. When their master learned of a kenku plot to steal a beautiful treasure, the entity imposed three dreadful punishments upon them.

- ➤ Their beloved wings were stripped away.
- ➤ Their creative spark was snuffed out.
- ➤ Their voices were stolen.

SIZE Kenku are smaller than humans, around five feet tall. They weigh between 90 and 120 pounds.

20

Haunted by an ancient crime that cursed their species, kenku wander the world as vagabonds and thieves. Stripped of their wings as retribution, all kenku are driven by the desire to fly once more. Many take up spellcasting in the hopes of achieving this dream, while others search the world for magical items rumored to give the gift of flight. They are drawn to the sky, flitting around tall towers or high on mountaintops. Unable to settle for long, they live temporarily on the fringes of other creatures' communities before their wandering spirit moves them along to the next patch of lost sky.

The curse has stolen the kenkus' creative spark. They can speak only in sounds that they have heard before, and they write, draw, or otherwise create only what they have already seen. Their individual names come from the sounds they can reproduce, while non-kenku use a description of this sound in place of a name. They have a talent for learning and memorizing details, making them excellent scouts and spies, and many earn their living by plagiarism and theft.

The most ambitious and daring of kenku may strike out on their own as adventurers. They dislike solitude and will partner eagerly with fellow heroes, mimicking the voices and words of their companions. Kenku are able to replicate humanoid languages along with sounds, and they often combine overheard phrases with natural noises to convey their meaning.

ATTRIBUTES

Expert Forgers Kenku have a mystical ability to duplicate the handwriting and craftwork of other creatures, making them excellent forgers.

Mimicry Kenku can impersonate sounds with eerie accuracy, including voices. Another creature would need to listen very carefully in order to detect that it's fake!

TABAXI

FELINE FIXATIONS All tabaxi have quirks that reflect their catlike natures. Some purr when pleased, others lash their tails angrily when upset. Some can't resist napping in a patch of sunlight, while others constantly fidget with a ball of yarn in their pocket.

SIZE Tabaxi are generally a little taller than humans, with the slender bodies and long winding tails of cats!

AGE Tabaxi age at the same rate as humans.

Somewhere beyond the charted world is a distant, sunbaked land of catlike people called the tabaxi. A rare few have wandered outside their borders in search of stories, secrets, and lore. Their curiosity is boundless but their interests can be fickle. One day they may feel driven to study the legend of a famous warlock, and the next they may seek buried pirate treasure. The world is a puzzle box full of surprises, and tabaxi want to uncover them all.

Naturally agile and charismatic, tabaxi make excellent performers, often traveling in troupes as actors, acrobats, jugglers, and minstrels. This arrangement allows them to constantly visit new places and meet new people, never settling anywhere for long. Of course, joining an adventuring party also gives opportunities for excitement and discovery.

Tabaxi believe they are the creation of a trickster god named the Cat Lord, who imbues them with their catlike qualities and watches over them on their travels.

ATTRIBUTES

Claws Tabaxi can deliver a dangerous strike from their hands or feet, or clamber up walls and other surfaces with ease.

Nimbleness Tabaxi usually land on their feet, and can move extra fast when circumstances demand it— useful for making a quick getaway.

Stealth Tabaxi have a knack for slinking into shadows and observing from the darkness.

Perception Tabaxi can see in the dark and are unusually alert to the presence of others.

TIEFLING

TIEFLING NAMES Some tieflings are given names that reflect their infernal heritage and bring to mind dark magics. Others are named after a virtue or ideal, hoping they will live up to the values embodied by their moniker.

AGE Tieflings age at the same rate as humans and live a little longer.

SIZE Tieflings are similar in size than humans, although their horns and imposing auras may make them seem taller than they are!

DO YOU SOMETIMES FEEL LIKE YOU DON'T FIT IN?

ARE YOU USED TO RELYING ONLY ON YOURSELF TO GET THINGS DONE?

DO YOU TRUST THOSE CLOSE TO YOU, BUT KEEP OTHERS AT ARM'S LENGTH?

YOU MIGHT BE A **TIEFLING**!

Tieflings are not a true race, as they are not connected by a common bloodline. Instead, they are beings born to ordinary humans who have been touched by the darkest of magics.

With their long tails, horns, sharp teeth, and strange pupil-less eyes, tieflings are cursed to resemble devils. Some are defiantly proud of their appearance, decorating their horns or tails with jewels or precious metals, while others try to disguise these features. Their diabolical traits include a natural talent for magic.

Tieflings face considerable prejudice. They are often rejected by their communities, or even their families, so they head out into the world on their own, mistrusted by everyone they encounter. In turn, they tend to be distrustful of others as well.

Despite what superstitious strangers may think of them, tieflings are not inclined toward evil. Their cursed bloodlines determine their appearance, not their character. Yet, because of how they look, they are often denied work, lodging, or a fair chance to prove themselves. The life of an adventurer offers one path for tieflings determined to prove their virtue.

ATTRIBUTES

Presence Tieflings are noted for their magnetic charm. Even people who don't like or trust them will usually find them fascinating.

Fire Resistance Their infernal blood gives tieflings a natural resistance to fire and heat.

Hellfire Attacking a tiefling can be a dangerous gamble, as they can sometimes strike back instantly, consuming their attacker in flames!

Darkness Tieflings have the innate magical ability to create a cloud of shadow that's impenetrable, even to those with darkvision!

TORTLE

ARE YOU FRIENDLY AND
EASY TO GET ALONG WITH?

ARE YOU FASCINATED BY
THE BEAUTY AND VARIETY
OF NATURE?

DO YOU LOVE THE COMFORTS
OF HOME, BUT STILL WONDER
WHAT LIES BEYOND THE
HORIZON?

YOU MIGHT BE A **TORTLE!**

AGE Tortles live for about 50 years.
Their infancy lasts less than a year,
and they reach adulthood by age fifteen.
Tortles take a mate only in the final
years of their lives, and spend that time
raising their offspring in special fortified
hatcheries, preparing the young for
their lives ahead.

SIZE Adult tortles grow up to
six feet tall, but they are much
stockier and heavier than humans
of similar height, because of both
their thickset build and their dense
armored shells, which account
for about a third of their weight.

For tortles, life begins and ends on the beach—and the time in between is often spent there as well! This semiaquatic reptilian race of humanoids begins their lives hatched from eggs on a beach, and ends their lives protecting the eggs of the next generation. The tortoise-like shells on their backs are the only homes they will ever need, so they often live out in the wilderness, developing excellent survival skills such as fishing, hunting, and trapping.

Even-tempered and positive, tortles are always happy in their own company. They appreciate nature and solitude but also enjoy the comraderie of others and they love to make new friends.

Despite their general air of contentment, most tortles will experience a wanderlust at some point in their lives and head off to explore the world with nothing but their person. They're keen to see the variety of life and engage other cultures, though they will likely never settle anywhere for long, especially if they're expected to live with a roof above their heads.

UNDER DAY AND NIGHT Tortles believe that day and night watch over them, with the sun and the moon being the "eyes" of these protective forces. Any time both can be seen in the sky is considered blessed, and tortles are nervous when neither is visible. And they hate being underground!

ATTRIBUTES

Protection Tortles don't wear armor, but their shells offer a robust natural defense, and they can disappear into their shells for extra protection.

Strength Carrying a heavy shell everywhere really helps build the muscles!

Holding Breath Tortles cannot breathe underwater, but they can hold their breath for up to an hour—a useful talent for sea fishing, but also handy when there's poison in the air.

Claws The sharp claws of a tortle, paired with their natural strength, can do some serious damage.

BARBARIAN

FIGHTER

MONK

PALADIN

RANGER

ROGUE

CHARACTER CLASSES

The class you choose for your character is more than a profession—it's a calling! Classes shape not only what they can do, but what kind of person they are, as well as the way your character thinks about the world and interacts with others. For example, a barbarian might see the world as a constant struggle for survival, where brute strength and cunning are all that matter, while a paladin would filter interactions through the lens of faith, always aware of the holy battle between good and evil. A rogue would have contacts among thieves, spies, and other nefarious types, while a ranger would know foresters and innkeepers spread across the wild lands.

Your class provides special features, such as a fighter's mastery of weapons and armor, or a rogue's expertise with stealth. When you first start out, your skills won't be specialized, but as you gain experience, your character will grow and change, unlocking new abilities and powers. Choose your class wisely, for it will shape the hero you become!

BARBARIAN

PRIMAL PATHS Although all barbarians share a rage they call upon in times of need, where that anger comes from and how they feel about it can be quite different. Some barbarians consider their anger a curse, others see it as a blessing. Depending on what their belief entails, a barbarian may prescribe to a certain primal path.

PATH OF THE ANCESTRAL GUARDIAN
Ancestral Guardians communicate with powerful warriors from the past to gain strength from them in combat. Ancestral Guardians are part of a great lineage.

PATH OF THE BERSERKER
Berserkers thrill at combat and let their anger overwhelm them in a joyous display of violence. They're dangerous and effective.

PATH OF THE TOTEM WARRIOR
Totem Warriors accept a spirit animal as a guide, protector, and inspiration. The barbarian's rage is a gift given to them as part of their journey to enlightenment.

Barbarians are warriors of rage. They call upon deep wells of anger from within or draw on the fury of their ancestral spirits to grant them power and strength in their times of need. When your enemies outnumber you and things look lost, a barbarian's fearless combat abilities can turn the tide.

During combat, barbarians will charge into the fray without any hesitation. They know their place is up front, making sure all eyes are on them as they scream a war cry or roar with unmatched fury.

A barbarian's intense emotions guide their actions. Some are very protective of their communities and stay close to home, while others wander far in search of adventure and the thrill of battle.

EQUIPMENT AND ATTRIBUTES

Armor Barbarians wear light or medium armor (see pages 80 and 82). They want to make sure that any armor they do wear won't impede their movement in battle.

Weapons Barbarians tend to have large and loud weapons that work well with their rage-fueled attacks—hammers, battle axes, two-handed swords, and the like. They appreciate weapons that intimidate their foes and make them look even more fearsome than they already are.

Rage Barbarians have a primal ferocity they call upon in times of great stress. This rage helps them focus their attacks and enhance their strength. It also helps them shrug off blows and ignore pain for as long as their fury lasts. A raging barbarian is a scary sight to behold if they're your enemy, but their courage and passion in the heat of battle is also very inspiring to their allies.

Danger Sense Barbarians may seem reckless, but their senses are quite sharp. They're deeply in touch with their emotions and intuition, and it gives them an uncanny sense of when things around them aren't as they should be. When a barbarian perceives something wrong, get ready!

WULFGAR THE WARHAMMER

TEMPERED RAGE Like all barbarians, Wulfgar calls upon his internal anger to aid him in battle and shrug off wounds, but Wulfgar is not the type to relish these moments of rage. The time he spent with Bruenor Battlehammer (see page 36), a dwarven fighter who started as his enemy but over time became like a father to him, taught Wulfgar a lot about self-control and honor in battle.

Wulfgar is a famous human barbarian warrior who grew up in a northern land called Icewind Dale. As a member of the Tribe of the Elk, he learned how to hunt, forage, survive harsh winters, and defend his people from creatures and invading armies.

Facing Wulgar in combat is a terrifying prospect—he stands almost seven feet tall and weighs 350 pounds. His strength is incredible to behold, especially when swinging Aegis-Fang, his magical warhammer. With that mythic weapon at his side, Wulfgar has driven back invaders and defeated dragons. Facing Wulfgar head-on is a recipe for disaster, so only the most agile and careful have a chance of holding their own against him.

PLAYING WULFGAR
Wulfgar is not subtle or careful. He's direct, focused, confident, and always ready for combat. Growing up in a barbarian tribe has left him without much knowledge of cities, especially those in the south, and he feels ill at ease around too many people. Wulfgar thrives in cold open air and it is where he feels most at home.

AEGIS-FANG

Aegis-Fang is a legendary weapon for a legendary warrior. Forged by Bruenor Battlehammer and imbued with powerful dwarven magic, the head of the hammer is made from pure mithral with a diamond coating magically adhered during the forging process and an adamantine shaft. Its head is engraved with the magical inscriptions of Clangeddin, the dwarven god of battle, as well as the symbols of Moradin, the dwarven god of creation, and Dumathoin, keeper of secrets under the mountain.

Most people would have difficulty even lifting Aegis-Fang, but Wulfgar is well trained with the weapon and able to swing it with ease. Even more amazing, it will magically return to Wulfgar's hand at his command, allowing him to throw it at enemies and then get right it back, pummeling those who dare to stand in his way.

FIGHTER

DO YOU LIKE THE IDEA OF
CHARGING INTO BATTLE?

ARE YOU UP FRONT AND
READY FOR ACTION?

CAN YOU KEEP A COOL HEAD
WHEN THINGS GET INTENSE?

YOU MIGHT MAKE A GOOD
FIGHTER!

MARTIAL ARCHETYPES

With so many different fighters
out there, having a focal point
for your skills can be valuable.
There are many archetypes, but
here a few examples to help
inspire you.

BATTLE MASTER
These fighters carry on enduring
traditions of combat and weapon
mastery passed down through
generations. Studying the techniques
of the past gives them knowledge
they bring to future conflicts.

CHAMPION
These fighters focus on raw power
and strength, honing their physical
prowess to deadly perfection.

ELDRITCH KNIGHT
These fighters supplement their
battle skills with a bit of magic
knowledge, wielding spells that can
enhance their abilities and surprise
their enemies.

S oldiers, warriors, gladiators, mercenaries, bodyguards—there are as many different types of fighters as there are conflicts needing to be fought with weapon in hand. What all of these occupations share is a mastery of melee combat and a desire to stare down death and not give up.

Fighters encompass a wide range of combatants. There are those who use size and strength to gain the upper hand in battle, yet a number are dexterous or stealthy. Some are adept at long-range fighting with bows or spears, while others wade into hand-to-hand combat with a sword and shield, a polearm, or any other weapon in which they're trained. Whatever their methods or equipment, fighters are almost always at the front line of combat, charging forward to engage their enemies and protect their friends from harm.

EQUIPMENT AND ATTRIBUTES

Armor Fighters are trained to wear any type of armor, from light cloth or hide all the way up to full plate with a shield. Whatever is required, a fighter can wear it.

Weapons Fighters are trained with all regular and martial weaponry, giving them a deep pool from which to choose. Many also have specialized training with unusual weapons, so feel free to get creative.

Second Wind After long days of adventure and combat, when most other adventurers would be exhausted and lose momentum, fighters can dig deep within themselves to regain their strength and keep going. Their resolve inspires the rest of their group to push past adversity.

BRUENOR BATTLEHAMMER

MASTER BLACKSMITH More than just a warrior, Bruenor is also a brilliant smithy, able to forge powerful dwarven weapons from even the most difficult materials. The art of crafting a weapon from raw materials and building each component to its proper strength and balance is his lifelong pursuit. Bruenor trained for many years to understand how weapons are made, and it gives him a greater appreciation for how they're used in combat.

Bruenor Battlehammer is a famous dwarven fighter known for his gruff demeanor and impressive fighting skills. Loyal to his friends and vicious to his enemies, Bruenor longed for the day when he and his people could reclaim their ancestral home, the dwarven fortress known as Mithral Hall, from the evil shadow dragon known as Shimmergloom. In time, Bruenor would find a way to make that dream a reality, and it would lead him to be crowned King of Mithral Hall.

In his prime, Bruenor was known for wearing a one-horned helmet, wielding a single-bladed axe, and carrying a shield emblazoned with a foaming mug sigil (the symbol of Clan Battlehammer).

PLAYING BRUENOR Bruenor is abrupt and stubborn, even more so than regular dwarves, who are already known for their dour attitude. In conversation, he doesn't waste time, and that direct approach carries through all his interactions, social and physical.

A headstrong curmudgeon, Bruenor is hard on his friends and family, expecting them to do their best no matter what situation they find themselves in. He's just as hard on himself, pushing his physical limits and charging first into battle so others don't get hurt. Bruenor is a true hero, courageous and caring, even if he doesn't let it show on the surface.

FLAMETONGUE

Bruenor's magic axe, Flametongue, bursts into flame upon his command, creating light and burning foes even as its blade cuts deep. Bruenor becomes the center of attention in combat when he fearlessly raises Flametongue as magical fire pours forth; allies rally around as they rush into battle. A dwarven army at Bruenor's command is an awe-inspiring sight on the battlefield.

MONK

DO YOU WANT TO HARNESS THE MYSTICAL POWER THAT LIES WITHIN?

ARE YOU NIMBLE YET STRONG?

CAN YOU HANDLE THE RIGORS OF A MONASTIC LIFE?

YOU MIGHT MAKE A GOOD MONK!

MONASTERY LIFE Monasteries are typically small, walled communities where monks live a simple, structured life focused on training, study, and, sometimes, farming. While some compounds are isolated, others interact freely with their neighbors, trading their services for food and goods.

Many monks enter the monastery as children, sent to live there because they had been orphaned or their parents could no longer feed them. Others are sent by their parents in gratitude for some service the monks had performed to help their family.

Monks dedicate their lives to the study of a mystical force called ki, which flows through all living creatures in the world. They learn to harness this energy within their own bodies, channeling it into powerful blows and elegant dodges that display uncanny speed and strength. These graceful fighters shun complex weapons and armor, relying upon the power that lies within to achieve their victories!

The life of a monk begins in childhood, when they live in tight-knit communities and their daily training follows a rigid routine. Becoming an adventurer means leaving this structure behind, a harsh transition that few undertake lightly. Adventuring monks generally do not value gold or glory, focusing instead on the pursuit of self-improvement and spiritual enlightenment.

EQUIPMENT AND ATTRIBUTES

Armor Monks choose not to wear any type of armor, since it interferes with the flow of ki.

Weapons Monks can use simple weapons and short swords. They favor inexpensive weapons such as staffs and clubs that can move with the flow of their martial attacks.

Ki A monk's training allows them to harness the mystical power of ki. This energy allows them to make extra unarmed blows after an attack, improve their ability to dodge, or even disengage from battle with a powerful jump. In the beginning, access to ki is limited, but as monks become more skilled, the amount of ki they harness also grows. Experienced monks are capable of astonishing, supernatural feats using their ki!

Martial Training Most monks begin training in the martial arts at a young age. They may have studied broadly, gaining a basic competence in a wide range of fighting styles, or chosen to focus their training on a single skill, mastering a specific weapon or unarmed attack. Their training emphasizes a flowing, dexterous approach to combat; witnessing a monk in battle is like watching a complex, elegant dance.

WHEY-SHU

SHADOW STEP Whey-Shu's control over shadows allows her to physically move between them, stepping into the darkness on one side of a room and emerging on the other. In a fight, she can teleport between shadows, disorienting her opponents as she unleashes quick strikes from different locations!

CLOAK OF SHADOW Through the power of her ki, Whey-Shu can become one with the darkness. Unless in a very brightly lit space, she can magically wrap shadows around her body, concealing her from view. In combat, she uses this ability to devastating effect, striking unseen and then vanishing again before her opponent can land a single blow!

PLAYING WHEY-SHU Whey-Shu is quiet but confident, willing to let others talk while she observes and plans. Once she decides to act, she is swift and determined. Her goal is to end a conflict as quickly as possible. If she miscalculates her enemy's strength, she will retreat and reassess before trying again. What matters most to her is the result, not individual setbacks along the way.

There is a famous kenku monk known as Whey-Shu, but that's not her actual name. It's just the closest sound most humanoids can make to her true name, the sound of a soft slipper sliding across a wooden floor. Whey-Shu's name reflects both her monastic training and her quiet presence, behind which she conceals considerable power.

After her kenku flock was saved from a goblin invasion by dwarven monks, Whey-Shu's parents gave her, their youngest child, to the monastery in gratitude. Her inability to communicate relegated her to the role of a lowly servant, and she was assigned to cleaning duties and making copies of sacred texts. Her kenku gift for mimicry soon led her to spend nights practicing the techniques from the scrolls she spent the day transcribing. By the time the monks discovered Whey-Shu's secret training regiment, she had developed incredible control over ki power that rivaled many adults. Despite her youth, Whey-Shu is now widely regarded as one of the masters of the Way of the Shadow, a monastic tradition that emphasizes stealth and subterfuge.

THE WAY OF THE SHADOW

One monastic tradition focuses on the use of ki energy to manipulate shadows and darkness—the Way of the Shadow. Known as shadowdancers, such monks often serve as spies and assassins. Like mercenaries, they are hired by any who can afford their fees. Whey-Shu doesn't mind working for others for money. The one exception is fighting goblins—she still has vivid memories of the invasion that endangered her family and eagerly battles goblins free of charge.

PALADIN

DO YOU LONG TO SERVE
A NOBLE CAUSE?

ARE YOU EQUALLY HAPPY
HELPING FRIENDS AND
SMITING ENEMIES?

DO YOU WANT TO BE THE
BEST AT BEING GOOD?

YOU MIGHT BE A PALADIN!

SACRED OATHS Paladins use magic with power derived from a commitment to their gods. To that end, all paladins must swear a holy oath that grants them special spells and abilities. If paladins fail to live up to their pledge, they may be cut off from these powers.

OATH OF THE ANCIENTS
Paladins who take this oath are dedicated to love and kindness. They have the power to channel the wrath of nature and use other nature-based spells.

OATH OF DEVOTION
Paladins who take this oath are dedicated to the causes of honesty, virtue, and compassion. They can bless their weapons and use spells of protection and revelation.

OATH OF VENGEANCE
Paladins who take this oath are dedicated to punishment and retribution. They can grant themselves advantage in battle and use other spells to help destroy their enemies.

Some adventurers seek glory, some seek wealth, and some seek excitement, but paladins pursue a life of adventure in service to a higher calling. They are warriors and champions of righteousness who fight the wicked and save the innocent because they've been called by their god or gods to do so. And their gods imbue them with divine gifts to make them better servants. However, if a paladin ever fails to live up to their gods' ideals, they may find their divine powers leaving them.

Paladins are skilled warriors with expertise in many weapons and fighting styles, but they're also adept spellcasters who channel the power of their gods to help or heal those around them, or to smite their foes with a single devastating blow. Paladins are typically very disciplined fighters who head into battle with clear purpose and unshakeable principles.

EQUIPMENT AND ATTRIBUTES

Armor Like fighters, paladins are trained to wear any type of armor, from light cloth or hide all the way up to full plate with a shield.

Weapons Paladins are trained with all regular and martial weaponry, so they have many options when heading into battle.

Healing Touch Paladins are blessed with the ability to heal wounds, cure disease, or remove poisons by laying on hands. Paladins are immune to disease because of the power flowing through them.

Divine Powers Devotion to their gods gives paladins special abilities, including the power to sense whether a person is wicked or good and the power to channel divine energy into a strike known as Divine Smite. Some paladins can also project an aura that protects or inspires those around them.

Martial Prowess Paladins are soldiers of faith, and they are well trained in the ways of battle. Some choose to be great defensive fighters, protecting those in trouble. Others choose to be great offensive fighters, putting all their energy into smiting!

REDCLAY

CLEANSING FIRE As a dragonborn with fire dragon ancestry, Redclay was born with the ability to breathe fire, but as a master paladin she has a much more devastating ability. For brief periods of time, Redclay can surround herself, and her allies, with a wall of divine flame that destroys nearby enemies while leaving those enclosed untouched by the blaze.

PRAYER OF HEALING Redclay is a devotee of Bahamut, the draconic god of justice. Through her prayers to him, Redclay can heal the sick and injured. She offers particular care to those afflicted by madness or delusion, believing the mad should be restored, not punished.

An orphan dragonborn raised in a remote mountain monastery dedicated to the draconic god Bahamut, Redclay first came to notice one brutal winter when her home was besieged by an army of orcs seeking control of the mountains. A month into the siege, with food almost all gone, Redclay slipped out of the monastery and passed through the enemy camp undetected. She returned leading an army of Bahamut faithful and headed a cavalry charge that broke the siege apart. She was 13 years old.

After becoming a celebrated figure, Redclay was named a general of her clan. Yet she found that neither the life of a soldier nor the life of a monk quite suited her, so she became a paladin, seeking out those most in need of aid and giving them hope when all seemed lost.

Though still quite small for a dragonborn, and so youthful that she retains her childhood name, Redclay is widely respected for the strength of her faith and the scale of her accomplishments.

PLAYING REDCLAY
Redclay is a devout and humble warrior who lives a simple life of service to others. Her chosen cause is to help people of good character who are suffering from injustice and have nowhere else to turn. Though she is content to pursue her crusade alone, she will gladly accept the aid of traveling companions if they are also above repute. She will always put the needs of others ahead of her own.

THE WAR DRUM OF BAHAMUT

Redclay's fame makes her an inspiring figure, but she also possesses a drum, given to her by the monks, that can magically inspire all those who fight at her side. Any ally of Redclay within earshot when she plays the drum before battle receives a boost to their courage that makes them fearless and resistant to mind control during the fight.

RANGER

ANIMAL COMPANIONS

While some rangers prefer to be solitary hunters, many find friendships with animals in their travels, and some even form lasting fellowships with these animal allies. Here is a short list of possible animal companions.

BADGER
Quick, able to burrow, and has a sharp sense of smell.

BAT
Able to fly, can locate things in the dark, and has a keen sense of hearing.

BOAR
Can charge and attack with their sharp tusks.

CAT
Quick, athletic, and has sharp claws.

GIANT WOLF SPIDER
Can spin webs, climb walls, and sneak around.

LIZARD
Quick, stealthy, and can give a nasty bite.

OWL
Able to fly, keen hearing and sight, and has sharp talons.

PANTHER
Sneaky, able to pounce, and has sharp claws and teeth.

RAT
Tiny and easily able to hide, can see in the dark, and has an annoying bite.

WOLF
Keen sense of smell and hearing, with a strong, powerful bite.

angers are hunters, scouts, trappers, or nomads. They're warriors of the wilderness who specialize in stopping monsters that threaten civilization. Rangers feel comfortable in nature and can befriend local wildlife, but when it comes to taking down a specific target, they can be deadly and unrelenting.

In combat, rangers know how to use the immediate environment to their advantage. Any tree can be a hiding spot as they sneak up on their prey. Every field can be used to set a trap or snare. With practice, rangers learn how to wield simple nature spells to enhance their stealth, increase their speed, or strengthen their focused attacks.

EQUIPMENT AND ATTRIBUTES

Armor Rangers tend to wear light or medium armor (see pages 80 and 82) so they don't impede their movement or make too much noise.

Weapons Rangers prefer quick weapons to large and bulky ones. Swords, spears, knives, and axes in close combat and bows for ranged combat are the norm. Some rangers specialize in nonlethal capture of their prey, in which case they may use ropes, nets, snares, and even darts with mixtures that knock out their targets.

Favored Enemy Almost all rangers choose a type of monster on which to focus their hunting skills. Some rangers build their entire identity around hunting specific beasts—giant killers, dragon hunters, demon stalkers, or vampire slayers.

Natural Explorer Rangers may also specialize in making the most of a particular type of terrain: arctic, desert, forest, grassland, mountain, swamp, or the strange subterranean land known as the Underdark. Once the ranger enters their preferred environment, that training kicks in and they can be even more effective.

LEGENDARY RANGER

MINSC THE MIGHTY

PLAYING MINSC Minsc is unwavering in his desire to battle evil and he will never back down from fighting for what he believes is good and right, even against enemies many times his size. He is fearlessly courageous, almost to the point of being suicidal. Everything Minsc does, he throws himself into with reckless abandon.

The legendary ranger is an eternal optimist, believing the best of himself, his allies, and everything around him. In Minsc's mind, the world is a very simple place of heroes and villains—either you're good or you're evil. Everyone he considers good should be his friend and everyone he considers evil needs a swift boot in the butt. Minsc's quest to prove he's a legendary hero never ends.

Minsc, and his hamster animal companion Boo, are fabled heroes known throughout a well-traveled part of the land called the Sword Coast. Over the years they have "kicked butt for goodness" many times, defeating monsters big and small while saving lives and building their reputation as great heroes.

The legendary ranger and his hamster are more than 100 years old thanks to an unexpected turn of events. During one of their adventures, the two were turned into a statue by evil magic and then, many decades later, turned back to flesh and blood. Minsc has always been a bit confused about where he is or who his friends are, and this bizarre time shift has only served to enhance his discombobulation.

BOO THE HAMSTER

Minsc is absolutely convinced that Boo is more than the small rodent he appears to be. Minsc tells his allies (and anyone else who will listen) that Boo is a "miniature giant space hamster," which sounds impressive but doesn't make a whole lot of sense. Whether or not Boo has this impressive lineage, he's definitely smarter than the average hamster and is capable of impressive problem solving. What's also apparent is that Boo is fiercely loyal to Minsc and, when things are dire, quite proficient at viciously fighting to defend his closest friend. An angry Boo will rapidly race around his opponent, biting, scratching, and attacking vital areas, including eyes, ears, the nose, and even "down below." Most enemies assume a hamster is not much of a threat, but a bum-bite from Boo quickly changes their minds.

ROGUE

DO YOU LIKE HIDING IN SHADOWS AND SURPRISING FRIENDS AND FOES?

ARE YOU SPEEDY INSTEAD OF STRONG?

IS YOUR MIND AS NIMBLE AS YOUR FINGERS?

YOU MIGHT MAKE A GOOD ROGUE!

THIEVES AND ASSASSINS When you have a reputation for sneaking around, picking locks, and going where you're not welcome, it's easy to see why common folk consider rogues as criminals. In many cases, they're not wrong. Many rogues break the law and take things that aren't theirs, but not all of them are evil. Some rogues do what they do for the thrill of adventure, enjoying the challenge of solving puzzles and exploring dangerous places.

Rogues are problem solvers. They rely on stealth and dexterity over big weapons and bigger muscles. When you need to get in somewhere without making a sound, pick a complex lock on a treasure chest, or set off a deadly trap without anyone getting hurt, you call in a rogue.

When it comes to combat, rogues rarely charge into battle. Remember, they're not fighters or paladins. A rogue would rather sneak up on a bad guy and make a precise strike that will impair the target. Successful rogues are versatile and resourceful, always looking for a solution that keeps them out of danger while getting them closer to filling their pouches with gleaming treasure.

EQUIPMENT AND ATTRIBUTES

Armor Rogues wear light armor (see page 80) so they can keep moving quickly while staying quiet.

Weapons Rogues tend to use small and fast weapons—daggers, rapiers, short swords, small crossbows, and so on. They value weapons that they can easily conceal and pull out at a moment's notice.

Sneak Attack Rogues specialize in distracting or surprising enemies in order to strike them in a vulnerable spot. In combat, rogues leave the loud and flashy attacks to their heavily armored friends while moving in from the sidelines like a cat ready to pounce at the perfect time.

Thieves' Cant Rogues have their own special form of communication. A combination of hand movements, facial expressions, symbols, and slang, it allows them to carry on a conversation without non-rogues knowing what they're really talking about. It's a good tool for gaining information in a seedy part of town or helping out a friend who shares the same profession.

SHANDIE FREEFOOT

TRICK SHOTS Shandie's skill with a bow has reached such incredible levels that she can fire arrows into darkness and hit her target based solely on sound, or shoot into a windstorm and compensate for the violent changes in trajectory. Once Shandie sets her mind to hitting a target, her arrows almost always find their mark.

BOWYER AND FLETCHER

Shandie decided she didn't just want to master firing a bow, she wanted to understand every aspect of its creation. She studied how to craft her own bow from a single piece of wood and even whittle her own arrows. Controlling every part of the process has given Shandie even more confidence with her favorite weapon.

Shandie Freefoot is an infamous thief and archer based in Baldur's Gate, a coastal city with a reputation for secrets and scoundrels. She grew up on the rough and tumble streets of the Lower City and quickly learned that if she wanted to survive, she needed to be fast on her feet and even faster with her wit and weaponry. The first time Shandie saw a bowman gracefully launch an arrow into a bull's-eye, she knew she had to master archery. Halfling elders told her that her small size would make it too difficult to carry a bow and strike targets across a battlefield, but she took that as a challenge. With years of practice, Shandie learned how to rapidly climb to high vantage points and effortlessly fire arrows while constantly staying on the move. Any opponents underestimating this stealthy halfling rogue soon realize how dangerous she is as a volley of arrows bear down on them from unexpected rooftops or shadowy corners.

PLAYING SHANDIE Shandie is confident and cool under pressure. She's been through enough scrapes to know that she can figure a way out of almost any situation. Once she draws back an arrow and prepares to fire, she is completely focused, holding perfectly still while she decides how much speed and power she'll need to strike her target.

THE QUIVER OF EHLONNA

Over the course of her adventures, Shandie acquired a magical quiver. A regular quiver can hold approximately twenty arrows and weighs about 2 pounds. The Quiver of Ehlonna looks like a well-crafted piece of equipment, but few people realize it can hold up to sixty arrows in the exact same space and with the same weight as a normal quiver. When Shandie draws an arrow, the quiver magically replenishes, keeping her well stocked in combat and surprising foes who assume she's run out of ammunition.

CLASS FLOWCHART

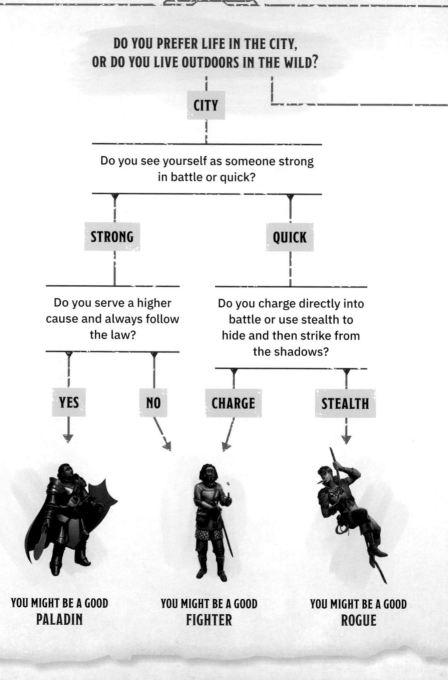

**DO YOU PREFER LIFE IN THE CITY,
OR DO YOU LIVE OUTDOORS IN THE WILD?**

CITY

Do you see yourself as someone strong
in battle or quick?

STRONG

QUICK

Do you serve a higher
cause and always follow
the law?

Do you charge directly into
battle or use stealth to
hide and then strike from
the shadows?

YES

NO

CHARGE

STEALTH

YOU MIGHT BE A GOOD
PALADIN

YOU MIGHT BE A GOOD
FIGHTER

YOU MIGHT BE A GOOD
ROGUE

Choosing a character class can be difficult, so here's a little chart you can use to help you decide.

OUTDOORS

Do you see yourself as someone angry in battle or more calm?

ANGRY

CALM

Do you launch a head-on assault in battle, or are you more strategic in order to keep your opponent off guard?

Do you enjoy being in nature and with animals, or do you prefer to be alone with your thoughts?

ASSAULT

STRATEGIC

NATURE

ALONE

YOU MIGHT BE A GOOD
BARBARIAN

YOU MIGHT BE A GOOD
RANGER

YOU MIGHT BE A GOOD
MONK

CHARACTER BACKGROUND & INSPIRATION

Characters are more than just their race or class; they're individuals with their own special stories to be told. You get to decide where your hero came from and how their experiences have led them to this point. Here are a few sample background ideas to help inspire your concept. You can use one of these or create your own.

ACOLYTE Your character was raised in a temple and knows the sacred rites and customs. Are you still friends with the church? Do you go on quests to raise funds for them?

CRIMINAL You've been a troublemaker for a long time and have struggled to stay on the right side of the law. Are you still committing crimes, or are you trying to mend your ways? Do you have criminal contacts who might still be looking for you?

ENTERTAINER You thrive when there's an audience in front of you looking for entertainment. What kind of performance do you specialize in—dance, music, poetry, singing, or something else? Are you just getting your start, or are you well-known for your art form?

FOLK HERO You may come from a small village or far-off town, but you're already starting to gain a reputation as a person who others look to in their time of need. What did you do in the past to gain this reputation? What heroic deeds are you hoping to achieve in the future?

HERMIT You've lived away from towns and cities for a long time, whether that was in a monastery or completely on your own somewhere remote. What has brought you back from your isolation? Are you excited to reconnect with the rest of the world, or do you want to get back to solitude as soon as possible?

NOBLE You have a title and your family owns land or riches. They may also have local political influence. Is your family well-liked by the locals, or do they have a bad reputation? Do you enjoy being part of this famous family, or do you hide your family name from those you meet?

OUTLANDER You've grown up away from large populations and you feel most comfortable in the wilderness. What do you think of city dwellers? How do you deal with people who destroy forests or mine the land?

SAGE You've always felt more comfortable reading books and studying scrolls. You have a lot of knowledge, but you've yet to put it into practice in the wider world. What has prompted you to leave your books and go on an adventure? How do you feel about war and conflict?

SOLDIER War has always been a part of your life, whether as part of a mercenary company or a recruit in a full-size army. Either way, you understand armed conflict and following orders. Are you still hungry for battle, or has your opinion changed? Did you earn rank in an army, or did you desert your post?

URCHIN You grew up on the streets, orphaned and poor. You learned to fend for yourself and survive, all the while yearning for something more. What was the name of the city you grew up in? Do you still have contacts there and, if so, how do they feel about you now?

DETAILS &
WHAT MAKES YOU SPECIAL

Once you've figured out your main features and where your character came from, it's time to work out the details that will make them unique and interesting.

NAME Names are important. They create an impression and build expectations. A powerful-sounding name, like "Battlehammer," tells people you're a capable warrior, while a name such as "Fenius" can sound mysterious or sly. Silly or serious, bubbly or brutal, whatever you choose, make sure it's something that exemplifies the key traits of your character.

HEIGHT AND WEIGHT
You don't need to work out your exact height and weight, but it can be useful to know which races tend to be taller than others.

Every hero has a distinctive element that helps them stand out from the crowd. It might be something internal, like a secret they keep or a piece of ancient lore they discovered, or it might be external, like a special birthmark, an item they carry, or an expertise they have. When coming up with ideas for your character, figure out what makes them special while not overlapping too much with other characters. Everyone in the group deserves to have their own unique feature.

Give your character a big goal to accomplish or a faraway place to visit and you'll see how easy it can be to build a story around their adventures.

OTHER PHYSICAL CHARACTERISTICS

You can decide if your character is young or old, as well as the color of their skin, hair, and eyes. Speaking of hair—how much of it do they have and how short or long do they keep it? Do they have any tattoos, scars, or other markings?

Close your eyes and imagine how your character might look. The more distinctive and interesting you can make them, the better.

DON'T FORGET FLAWS

It may seem counterintuitive when you're creating someone heroic, but adding weaknesses can help make someone distinctive. It's fun to think about flaws and make them part of your character's personality.

Is your character afraid of something? Do they have something they hate? Are they dimwitted, quick tempered, disorganized, or scatterbrained? Are they allergic to cats, loose with their money, or do they have an old injury that gives them a hard time?

Give your character at least one flaw and you might be surprised at how enjoyable it can be to incorporate it into their history.

HATS

Headgear is available in a wide range of styles and sizes, from close-fitting rogue caps to huge, floppy wizard hats. Whatever the design, they're helpful for keeping sun and rain off the faces of weary adventurers trekking from dungeon to dungeon.

SHIRT

Some adventurers prefer loose shirts for mobility, and others like a more fitted garment that won't impede them while fighting. Either way, shirts can range from plain and rough to ultra-soft items made from the finest fabrics.

CLOAK

Part clothing, part blanket, a cloak is crucial for protecting you from bad weather, concealing you from enemies, and keeping you warm at night.

WAISTCOAT

Waistcoats are worn for reasons of warmth, style, and all those extra little pockets.

PANTS/SKIRT

Either pants or skirts are suitable for adventuring, so long as they are made from sturdy fabric and cut loose enough to allow a full range of movement. You can wear a skirt over leggings for added warmth.

FOOTWEAR

Boots are the most common footwear choice for adventurers, helping to protect your lower legs from water, slime, and ankle-biting beasts. Some adventurers prefer a soft-soled shoe that allows for extra-quiet footsteps.

CLOTHES: ANATOMY OF AN ADVENTURER'S OUTFIT

Clothing can say a lot about your character's personality, wealth, and social status. In turn, that affects how other characters, including allies and villains, respond to you. Fancy robes can help during negotiations with a local lord—or help you infiltrate that same lord's castle on a secret mission. Many magic users prefer long, loose garments with lots of hidden storage spots for their spell components and enchanted talismans. Some vestments are even covered with symbolic or magical designs. The tattered rags of a peasant might cause a warlock to hesitate when trusting you with an important quest—or allow you to pass through a crowd unnoticed by soldiers who are searching for you.

TRINKETS

Carried usually for sentimental reasons, trinkets are small objects that reflect your character's background and personality but aren't useful in combat (unless you're very creative!). They can also play a role in your interactions with other characters or provide the spark of inspiration for stories. Ideas include:

- A crystal that glows faintly in the moonlight
- A coin from an unknown land
- A tiny knife that belonged to a relative
- An empty vial that smells of perfume when opened

WHAT TO WEAR WHEN YOU'RE ADVENTURING!

Your choice of clothing can change how you move, how you fight, and how others interact with you. What you wear changes your style and strategy, so choose carefully.

THE CLASS MAKES THE CLOTHES!

Although adventurers are free to wear whatever they like, each class does lean toward certain types of clothing that best suits their abilities.

- **Barbarian** These fierce, primitive warriors prefer garments that maximize their ability to move quickly and inflict damage on their enemies. They value durability over decoration, although many carry tokens of their home tribes on their adventures.

- **Fighter** Highly trained combat specialists, the clothing of these classic warriors ranges from plain materials to colorful displays of their sworn allegiances.

- **Monk** Masters of the martial arts, these spiritual warriors rely solely on their body's defenses, favoring plain monastic robes that allow their ki to flow freely.

- **Paladin** These holy warriors prefer standard adventurer's garb, and they often incorporate symbols of their faith into their attire.

- **Ranger** These nature-based trackers and hunters favor muted shades that let them blend in to their forest environments.

- **Rogue** Stealth is important to rogues, who favor dark colors and garb that lets them move quiet and unseen through the world.

ADVENTURER'S CLOTHES

Durable clothes created to survive the varied dangers of a dungeon environment, including the cold and damp, or battle damage. Designed to be easily repaired, and often given a personal touch to help bolster an adventurer's spirit.

Wear this when trekking into dangerous environments—or to impress locals with tales of your past adventures.

Don't wear this when you need to stay out of sight. Adventurers attract attention, and not always the friendly kind.

FINE CLOTHES

Ornate attire made from expensive materials, which may even feature silk threads and gemstone decorations.

Wear this when you need to impress nobles, engage in diplomacy, or intimidate poor folks.

Don't wear this when you're out adventuring—fancy fabrics are too delicate for the dangers of a dungeon, and all that bling may attract nasty creatures!

TRAVELER'S CLOTHES

Sturdy, practical clothing in rough, but durable, fabric. Often features long cloaks for warmth and protection against the elements!

Wear this when you're traveling long distances or trying to find a spot at an inn.

Don't wear this to a fancy banquet, unless you want to upset your host.

EQUIPMENT

The right equipment is of paramount importance to an adventurer. The proper gear can mean the difference between life and death when trapped in a dungeon or while traveling across rugged lands. Weapons and armor seem obvious, but what about the other things you might need? Rope to climb steep cliffs and lockpicks to open sealed doors, a tinderbox to start fires and a bedroll to sleep on, a lantern to guide you through the dark and rations to keep you fed. You can't carry *everything*—that'd be far too heavy—so you'll need to pack carefully!

As you create your character, think about their background and where their equipment—or the gold to buy it—came from. Are you the only child of wealthy merchants, able to afford the best of everything, or did you come from humble beginnings, earning your gear through hard work and careful saving? Do you wear robes unique to the monastery where you were raised or possess a legendary axe inherited from a famous relative? Your equipment helps tell the story of who your character was before their adventure began and bolsters victory in your upcoming quests!

WEAPONS: BE READY FOR COMBAT

Whether you favor a longsword or a longbow, your weapon and your ability to use it effectively while adventuring will mean the difference between life and death. Your race and class can make you extra-effective with certain weapons or prevent you from using others, so you'll want to take both into consideration when making your choices.

Most people can use simple weapons without needing extra training. These include clubs, maces, and other arms often found in the hands of common folks. Martial weapons, including swords, axes, and polearms, require more specialized training. It's possible to injure yourself instead of an enemy if you attack with a weapon you don't know how to use, so watch out!

In addition to functionality, you should think about personal touches that make your weapons cool and unique. Is your axe engraved with dwarven runes? Does your dagger have a jeweled handle or a special scabbard? Was your shortbow's wood hewn from a sacred tree in far-off elvish lands? Your weapon will be your constant companion on the adventure ahead, so choose one you can trust!

SWORDS

The classic warriors' weapon, swords are made from a long piece of metal sharpened on both edges and mounted on a sturdy handle known as a hilt. They come in a range of lengths and weights and may be highly decorated or left plain, depending on the owner's wealth and taste.

Swords can be used to slash at enemies, puncture them with the sharp tip, and even deliver blunt strikes with the broadside or the hilt. The more ways your warrior can think of to wield their weapon, the harder it will be for enemies to dodge their attacks!

SHORTSWORD

Nimble and adaptable, shortswords are popular across most character classes. Their light weight makes them a great choice for long journeys, and their lower cost makes them a popular option for adventurers who are just starting out.

As a one-handed weapon, shortswords allow their user to carry a shield as well—an important consideration for warriors who are restricted from some of the tougher armor classes. Don't underestimate the damage a skilled hero can do with one of these swift, sharp implements at their side!

LONGSWORD

The versatile longsword offers a great balance between the speed of a shortsword and the hefty power of a greatsword. As a one-handed weapon, they permit a hero to deliver swift, sharp strikes while allowing for a shield as extra protection. Used with both hands, longswords focus the full brunt of a warrior's strength into punishing blows.

The longsword is a great choice when you're not certain what kind of danger you'll be facing. Whether you tangle with lots of smaller opponents who need to be taken down quickly or a mighty beast that can only be defeated with powerful hits, the longsword is ready to deliver!

GREATSWORD

The greatsword is a mighty weapon requiring immense strength and skill to use effectively. Any untrained heroes may wind up hurting themselves more than their opponents if they wade into battle with one of these!

A two-handed weapon, greatswords can deliver powerful blows, even killing lesser creatures with a single strike. Due to their size and expense, greatswords are associated with paladins, fighters, and barbarians, although any trained warrior with sufficient might may find one to be a welcome ally on the field of battle!

POLEARMS

Polearms consist of a staff, typically made of wood, topped with a metal spike or blade. A classic battlefield weapon, their broad reach makes them a great choice against larger opponents. Armies often place rows of soldiers armed with polearms as their first line of defense against attacking cavalry, goblin hordes, giants, and other foes.

As close-combat weapons, polearms' longer length allows a wider swing than swords, increasing your range and building speed for a more brutal impact. Combined with a steady stance, a polearm can deliver crushing blows; paired with nimble footwork, the blade becomes a flashing blur of stabs and slashes. What fighting style will your warrior choose?

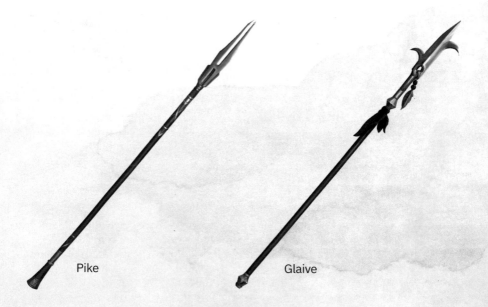

Pike

Glaive

PIKE Simple and effective, an inexpensive pike is a great weapon choice for starting heroes who find themselves short on gold. The spike delivers sharp stabbing damage to enemies, and can even be thrown if needed.

GLAIVE The curved hook of a glaive allows it to deal extra damage. You can even use it to snare opponents and pull them in close! The sharp edge of the blade can be used to stab or slash at foes for even more attack options.

HALBERD Combining the reach of a pike with the blade of an axe, a halberd opens up even more fighting techniques for a trained warrior. By gripping the staff near the base, you gain a wider range for your slashes, while holding it closer to the blade will deliver blows with a mighty impact.

FANG TIAN JI The complex blade of a fang tian ji is best placed in the hands of a highly trained fighter, for it takes years of experience to master the many attacks this weapon can achieve. Stabbing, slashing, even blunt impact from the flat side of the blade, this weapon will give you countless ways to overcome your foes.

Halberd

Fang Tian Ji

OTHER MELEE WEAPONS

Swords and polearms are common choices of weapons for adventurers who like to get close to the enemy, but other options are available, including axes, hammers, and whips! These weapons are often very simple, but also very effective.

AXES Originally intended to cut down trees and split wood, axes first became a popular weapon among forest-dwellers. Axes range greatly in size and style. Some have one blade, and some have two; a pickaxe has a blade on one side and a pick on the other.

Hand axes can be used as both melee and thrown weapons, and some adventurers learn how to wield two hand axes at once! Most axes are still primarily tools, but some of the most stylish axes, like the long-handled pole axe, are designed specifically as weapons.

FLAILS Flails were originally farmers' tools used to beat grain for harvesting, but farmers adapted them as weapons to defend against attackers. Basic flails consist of two wooden batons linked by a chain or rope. Sophisticated versions might include a blade, a metal claw, or a spiked metal ball on one or both ends. Martial artists may train all their lives to master the use of a flail.

HAMMERS Intended as tools for construction, demolition, and metalwork, hammers have become favored weapons among some of the hardiest races, including orcs and dwarfs, since they offer brutal power.

Hammers range in size from modest sledge hammers to huge iron mauls. Many are basic blunt instruments for striking enemies or denting armor, but warhammers are designed as impressive smashing weapons with long handles and small heavy heads to be wielded with speed and grace.

MACES Related to hammers, but conceived specifically as weapons, maces are metal bludgeons with spikes or blades designed to penetrate armor or pull a soldier off a horse. Because maces can be very ornate, they are sometimes the blunt weapon of choice for people of high status—but they can also be made from cheap raw iron and hit just as hard!

WHIPS Traditionally used for wrangling livestock, whips can be used as weapons by a highly trained expert. Some bullwhips extend as far as twenty feet, offering greater range than most melee weapons!

Other styles of whip have less reach but different advantages. Scourges are whips with multiple short tails that can be used to disarm an opponent. A riding crop can be carried discretely and delivers a stinging blow rather than lasting damage. Chain whips, made of metal rods linked by chains, are less flexible than other whips, but they hit very hard.

RANGED WEAPONS

Most ranged weapons were originally intended for hunting, but in a world of spellcasters, firebreathers, and terrible flying beasts, the ability to attack at long range can be a lifesaver. Bows and arrows are the most popular forms of ranged weapons, but they come in a few different styles, and there are some ranged weapons that might prove a better fit for your character.

BOWS Shortbows and longbows use the tension of a bowstring released by hand to propel an arrow toward a target. Shortbows are about three feet in height and can fire an arrow about eighty feet on average. Longbows are a couple of feet taller and can typically fire an arrow about one hundred fifty feet, but they're not as easy to carry around. All bows require some strength to use effectively.

CROSSBOWS Crossbows are simple mechanical weapons activated by pulling a trigger to release a catch on the bowstring, propelling a bolt toward a target. There are three popular types.

Hand crossbows are small and can be fired one-handed, but have a usual range of about thirty feet, and the string must be drawn back by hand. Light crossbows and heavy crossbows must be held two-handed, and a crank or lever is used to pull back the string. Light crossbows have a range of eighty feet, while a large and weighty heavy crossbow has a range of one hundred feet. Most crossbows can only fire one bolt at a time, and reloading can take several minutes.

DARTS (BLOW DARTS) Piercing darts can be thrown about twenty feet or shot from a blowgun to a distance of about twenty-five feet. Darts don't deliver much damage, so they are often tipped with dangerous or deadly poisons to make them more effective.

SLINGS A simple projectile weapon made of a pouch and cord, slings are used to fling a small blunt projectile with great force an average of thirty feet. Hard metal projectiles called "bullets" are often used, but one great advantage of a sling is that they can also launch found objects such as rocks or even coins!

THROWING WEAPONS Daggers, shurikens, and other bladed throwing weapons have a range of twenty to thirty feet, depending on their weight and design. They require great finesse and aim to use effectively.

SPECIAL WEAPONS

I f a sword or axe isn't your style, there are other options to consider. A unique "signature weapon" that matches your fighting style or history is one way your character might stand out from other adventurers.

BOOMERANG A thrown hunting weapon made of wood or bone that delivers a bludgeoning strike to a target. Expert users can throw a boomerang so that it returns to their hand, but only if it hasn't struck a target.

CHAIN Heavy iron chains are challenging weapons to wield, but if you have the strength to haul and swing a length of chain, you can hit hard!

NET Weighted fishing nets can be hurled at opponents, tangling them up and leaving them vulnerable to follow-up attacks.

PICK A small, sharp spike with a handle, traditionally used for breaking up ice or stone. Easily concealed, and effective in close-quarters combat.

PUSH DAGGER Another easily concealed close-quarters weapon, comprising a small stabbing blade and a horizontal handle that rests in the user's palm.

SCYTHE Originally designed for harvesting crops, scythes are long-handled tools with a curved horizontal blade used in a sweeping motion. Difficult to use as a weapon, but the blade can be reforged for use on a polearm or sword.

SICKLE A small one-handed version of a scythe. Its curved blade makes it a great choice for martial artists who strike at unexpected angles.

TRIDENT A spear with three prongs designed for spear fishing. A trident can be used as a throwing or thrusting weapon.

CRAZY COMBINATIONS

Instead of choosing a special weapon, you might take two familiar weapons and combine them in unusual ways. The only limits are your imagination! Here are some examples.

Dagger + Rope If you're an expert at throwing a dagger, adding a rope allows you to yank the dagger back.

Chain + Hammer A weighted chain with a bludgeon on the end creates an effective weapon for sweeping your enemies off their feet.

Crossbow + Axe Adding an axe blade to a crossbow creates a weapon that can be used for both ranged and melee combat.

Spear + Scythe Combining a spear and a scythe on either side of a pole creates a more versatile weapon for both forward and sideways attacks. Just remember to always check behind you!

Sword + Staff A sword can be hidden inside a staff or stick, giving you more options in combat and a chance to deliver a nasty surprise!

ARMOR: THE FOUNDATION OF A HERO'S DEFENSE

The toughest armor isn't always the best defense. Too much armor can slow down your character or even interfere with their magical abilities. Too little armor can leave you vulnerable to damage, especially if you tend to get up close and personal in a fight. Remember that some classes have restrictions on what kinds of armor they can use, so check what's available before you set your heart on that shiny suit of plate mail. Choose carefully if you want to survive the dangers ahead!

Budget is also a consideration for starting characters. Fancy metal armor can eat up all your savings, leaving you without the coins you'll need for food and additional gear. On the other hand, that homemade hide suit may be cheap, but it also won't offer much protection in a real fight. There's always a balance to be found when selecting armor.

GETTING IN (AND OUT) OF YOUR ARMOR

Putting on armor is no easy task. The speed with which you can go from normal clothes to full protection depends on the weight of your armor.

- **Light Armor** One minute

- **Medium Armor** Five minutes

- **Heavy Armor** Ten minutes

Make Your Choice Do you want to sit up for your turn keeping night watch in heavy, uncomfortable armor? Or, take the risk of having nothing but your weapon to protect you if there's an ambush? Luckily, it takes only a second to grab your trusty shield!

LIGHT ARMOR

Made from lightweight and flexible materials, light armor is the best choice for nimble adventurers. It will reduce damage from minor blows but might not be enough to protect you from stronger opponents.

PADDED ARMOR Made from quilted layers of cloth and batting, padded armor is lightweight and affordable, but not very strong. Be warned: This simple armor is bulky, which means your character is less stealthy than normal while wearing it.

Not ideal if you want to stay unnoticed.

LEATHER ARMOR The chest and shoulders of this armor are made of stiffened leather boiled in oil to increase its strength. The rest is made from softer materials that won't interfere with movement.

A great compromise between protection and weight, and pretty affordable too.

STUDDED LEATHER ARMOR This is leather armor that has been reinforced with rivets and spikes to help deflect blows.

Be careful, though—this type of armor is a lot more expensive than normal leather armor, and a lot heavier too. You don't want to wear this on a long trek unless you're quite strong.

CHOOSE WISELY

Remember, the more protection an armor provides, the more it interferes with your ability to move freely. If your character relies on being quick and agile, too much armor can actually be a bad thing.

MEDIUM ARMOR

Willing to sacrifice some mobility for extra protection? Medium armor may be just what you need. It's ideal for those who like to get into the thick of battle but possess more skills than just straightforward smashing to help them win the day.

HIDE Fit for a barbarian, this crude armor consists of thick furs and pelts that wrap around the body. Many evil humanoids also favor this type of protection.

CHAIN SHIRT Made of interlocking rings, a chain shirt provides modest protection. It's great at deflecting sharp blades, but less helpful against bashing damage from maces or hammers. Its rings can be loud when they clink together, so to muffle the noise it's best worn as a layer between your regular clothing and a leather outer shell.

SCALE MAIL This armor is a mixture of leather and metal pieces overlapping like the scales of a fish—hence its name. With a coat, leggings, gloves, and sometimes an overskirt, it provides full-body protection for the intrepid adventurer.

BREASTPLATE Combining the solid toughness of a metal torso with the flexibility of leather armor, a breastplate helps protect your vital organs without weighing you down too much. Be careful, though, your chest may be safe, but your arms and legs are still exposed.

HALF PLATE Covering most of the wearer's body, these shaped metal plates are held together by leather straps to ensure the armor stays in place throughout the toughest fight. This type of armor is very strong but does have open gaps that leave weak spots for a skilled opponent to target.

HEAVY ARMOR

This tough stuff is your best bet for getting through a rough fight unscathed. However, the weight and bulk of heavy armor means that only the strongest and most experienced of warriors can wear it in combat without encountering speed or movement difficulties.

RING MAIL

This is leather armor with heavy rings stitched across the surface. Metal makes it heavy to wear, but it's not as protective as chain mail because its rings are more spread out. On the plus side, it's less expensive than chain, making it a thrifty choice for beginning adventurers.

CHAIN MAIL

The interlocking metal rings over a layer of quilted fabric in this armor provides solid protection against sharp-edged weapons such as swords and arrows. Be careful, though, you can still bruise beneath chain mail, and the tiny rings can be noisy when moving around!

SPLINT ARMOR

Thin metal strips riveted onto leather backing create this tough, durable armor. Chain mail is added at the joints for extra protection at flexible spots, while thick padded fabric underneath keeps your skin from chafing.

PLATE MAIL

The classic armor of knights and adventurers, this huge metal suit is designed to provide protection from head to toe. You'll need thick padding underneath to protect your skin, and well-fashioned straps to keep the weight properly aligned over your whole body. And plate armor is loud, so forget sneaking up on most creatures while wearing this.

SHIELDS

Often, a shield is an adventurer's best friend. Capable of stopping a wide range of attacks, from swords and arrows to warhammers and whips, shields are quick and versatile defensive tools. You can even use them as a bludgeoning weapon if you're backed into a corner and disarmed.

SHIELD MATERIAL AND PARTS
Shields are made from many different materials, including wood, hardened leather, and metal. Wood and leather shields may have metal parts, like edges or spikes, to enhance their durability.

UMBO
A raised metal circle placed at the center of some shields, the umbo helps deflect blows aimed at the middle of the shield.

ENARMES
Leather-wrapped gripping handle attached to the back of the shield.

GUIGE
The long leather strap used to carry the shield across your back.

BUCKLER A small, round shield designed for basic personal protection, bucklers tend to be lightweight, inexpensive, and easy to carry and use. Their versatile design makes them the most common of all shields.

KITE Wide at the top and narrow at the bottom, kites are a longer shield that provides more coverage than a buckler. You can drive the pointed edge into the ground for added stability against an assault.

HEATER A smaller variation of the kite, a heater often has a peaked top to help defect sword blows. Its base is a little wider, giving more protection to the upper legs but potentially leaving your calves open to attack.

IMPROVISED Almost any object can become a shield with enough ingenuity—or desperation! Loose doors, coffin lids, metal serving plates, almost anything that's sturdy and in reach can help protect you from an enemy attack. You don't even need to be able to lift it—an overturned table or treasure chest makes a great place to hide from arrows! What kinds of improvised shields can you think of?

RUST MONSTER

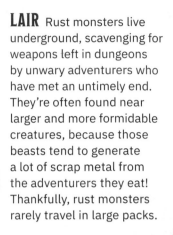

LAIR Rust monsters live underground, scavenging for weapons left in dungeons by unwary adventurers who have met an untimely end. They're often found near larger and more formidable creatures, because those beasts tend to generate a lot of scrap metal from the adventurers they eat! Thankfully, rust monsters rarely travel in large packs.

SPECIAL POWERS

SENSE METAL
Because rust monsters feed exclusively on metal, they can perceive ferrous metals up to fifty feet away. Single-minded in their pursuit of food, they may attack anyone who gets between them and dinner.

CORROSION
Rust monsters can corrode ferrous metals they touch and will destroy any vulnerable weapons used to attack them. The effects of their corrosion are irreversible, though some magical weapons and armors are immune to their powers.

SIZE Rust monsters resemble fleas, but you'll never find one on a dog. They're big enough to send most dogs running in the other direction! A fully grown rust monster is four to six feet long and weighs about 300 pounds.

The flealike giant insectoids called rust monsters are a terrible sight to encounter in the subterranean caverns they call home, but they're much more of a threat to your arms and armor than they are to you! Rust monsters feed on ferrous metals, which are any metals containing iron and vulnerable to rusting. That includes iron, steel, adamantine, and mithral.

There are much more dangerous creatures out there than these beasts (enough to fill a whole other book), but losing your equipment to a rust monster can leave you vulnerable to the next danger you encounter. For many adventurers, a run-in with a rust monster must be avoided at all costs, especially if said adventurers managed to buy or acquire the finest weapons available! Being very proud of their own ironwork, dwarves particularly hate rust monsters!

Some people keep rust monsters as pets—like a guard dog that's very effective against heavily armed intruders—but they need to be well fed, or they'll turn on your defenses!

DO THIS

Always carry at least one weapon that can't rust. A rust monster's hide is well-armored, so make sure the weapon you use is a tough one.

Dump your least valuable iron items in a rust monster's path. This may distract it as you run away. Many cooking pots have been lost in this manner.

DON'T DO THIS

Don't attack rust monsters. If you're not carrying any ferrous metals, they will happily ignore you.

Don't ever use your best iron or steel weapons to attack them. That is, unless those weapons are enchanted!

IN YOUR PACK: ITEMS FOR TRAVEL & EXPLORATION

Being a dungeon delver requires courage, a desire to explore, and the right tools for the challenges ahead. What you carry determines your success against tough terrain, worrisome weather, and creepy creatures.

Adventuring packs are an easy way to get all the gear you need for a particular task or quest, usually at lower cost than buying all the equipment individually. Your character class will probably inform the kind of starting equipment you'll want to take on your journey, and these packs might be just what you're looking for.

Even so, you can't take it all. Getting packed for an epic journey means making choices about what to bring and what to leave behind. Every bit of equipment or weaponry can slow you down, tire you out, or leave less room to carry the treasures you may find during your travels.

Use the information in this chapter to make a list of what you want to carry based on your class and its abilities, then outfit your heroic self and head toward adventure!

SURVIVAL GEAR

Whether crossing a desert, navigating a forest, or delving deep into a dungeon, there are certain things every adventurer needs to prepare for if they hope to survive, and that means bringing the right gear.

SHELTER The most basic form of shelter is a bedroll and a blanket but, if you can carry it, a weatherproof tarpaulin will help protect you from the elements. Better yet, bring a tent. Of course, some races are fine curling up in a tree or digging themselves a hole in the ground.

WATER A good waterskin is a vital piece of equipment for any adventurer, and you should take every opportunity to top up with clean drinkable water from a spring or stream.

FIRE Another vital piece of equipment is a tinderbox to light fires to keep you warm at night, cook food and boil water, and perhaps keep predators at bay. A tinderbox contains steel and flint, which can be struck together to create sparks, and some form of tinder, like wooden kindling or a flammable cloth, which can be used to ignite a fire.

LIGHT If you're navigating underground or by night, you'll need torches made from sticks wrapped in oil cloths that can be lit from a fire. Many adventuring races have darkvision, allowing them to see in low light, but this ability won't allow you to see colors in the dark.

FOOD Adventure food needs to be compact and durable. Hardtack biscuits, made with just flour and water, are a popular choice. These crackers keep for a very long time but taste terribly plain. If you can't pack enough food for a long journey or want something flavorful, hunting and fishing equipment are very useful, so long as you know what to do with them! A guidebook to safe foraging is also helpful, plus a cooking pot in which to prepare your meals.

NAVIGATION A magnetic compass will help you find your way through unfamiliar territory, though remember that iron-rich caverns can throw off its accuracy. If a map exists for where you're going, it's a good idea to bring that too.

FIRST AID A basic healer's kit contains bandages, lotions, and splints, all of which are very useful if you forgot to bring a healer for your party—or if your healer is the one injured!

ADVENTURING GEAR

Defeat the monster, get the gold, avenge the people, save the day—adventuring is about more than just survival. Getting past every obstacle and facing off against every threat requires special equipment, so acquiring the right adventuring gear is very important.

Adventuring gear is just about anything that might help you get to your goal, aside from weapons, armor, trinkets, and magical items. These are some of the most popular examples.

Climber's Kit + Rope

Component Pouch

Hunting Trap

Potion of Healing

AMMUNITION If your weapon of choice is a sling, a bow, or a blowgun, make sure you pack enough shots, arrows, bolts, or darts for the journey.

BALL BEARINGS The thief's favorite. A handful of ball bearings tossed on flat ground can create an instant tripping obstacle for anyone chasing after you!

CLIMBER'S KIT Whether you're scaling a cliff, a tree, or a castle wall, you'll be safer with a climbing kit that includes pitons, gloves, and a harness.

COMPONENT POUCH A leather pouch that hangs from your belt, with separate compartments to hold the items needed for a spell.

HUNTING TRAP A heavy iron trap that you can set on the ground to catch big beasts (or unwary foes).

POTION OF HEALING Never leave home without it!

ROPE Rope is very useful for climbing, but you can also use it for setting traps, swinging across a chasm, or tying up prisoners.

TOOLS

Whether you're picking locks, mixing potions, or performing for a crowd, you need the right tools for the job—and you need to know how to use them.

Tools are ordinary items associated with a craft, trade, or hobby. If you're playing a character who is supposed to be particularly good at a task, whether it's an honest woodworker or a cunning thief, you'll want to make sure you have the proper equipment.

Tools are often available in sets based around a profession. You should assume they contain everything you need to do that job, but none of the raw materials. For example, herbalist kits include a mortar and pestle, clippers, and pouches, but no plants. Jeweler kits include tiny pliers, hammers, and clamps, but no jewels.

POPULAR TOOL SETS

Alchemist's Supplies Includes a mortar and pestle, vials, flasks, and measuring spoons, so you can attempt to mix up potions or create precious metals.

Carpenter's Tools Includes hammers, saws, chisels, levels, and nails, but you'll have to fetch your own wood.

Cook's Utensils Includes a cooking pot, a pan, knives, and wooden spoons, as well as bowls to serve in. If you know how to use these items, you'll never be lonely on an adventure!

Disguise Kit Includes hair dye, makeup, and props to help you disguise or conceal your appearance.

Forgery Kit Includes papers, inks, and sealing wax to allow you to create convincing fake documents.

Gaming Set Includes dice, playing cards, and other game pieces that you can use to make friends—or enemies—in a local tavern.

Mapmaker's Tools Includes parchments, measuring tools, and inks, so you can always keep track of where you've been.

Musical Instruments Essential for every bard, whether it's a simple flute or a set of bagpipes.

Thief's Tools Includes lock picks, files, pliers, and a long-handled mirror. Great for opening locks and disabling traps!

BURGLAR'S PACK

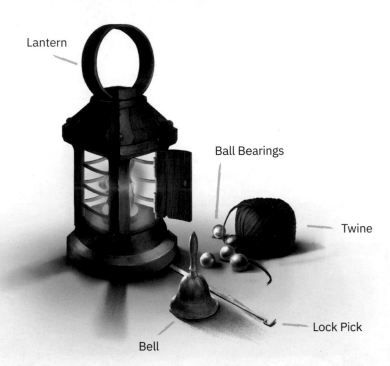

Lantern

Ball Bearings

Twine

Lock Pick

Bell

Burglars will tell you that what they do is an art; they're not just opportunistic thieves or rough hoodlums. They choose a target and go in quietly, taking only what they need and leaving the scene as undisturbed as possible.

A burglar's pack contains many of the essential tools of the trade, including a lantern that can be covered quickly, a bell that can be attached to twine to warn of passing patrols, a lot of rope, some ball bearings, and a crowbar and hammer for cracking locks. Of course, expert burglars may leave those last two behind if they know how to use a set of lock picks.

DUNGEONEER'S PACK

Wooden Torch

Crowbar

Backpack

You'll hopefully encounter a lot more dungeons than dragons in your adventures, and a dungeoneering pack contains the basic equipment for venturing down into the dark in search of treasure, including a backpack, a tinderbox, rope, climbing pitons, hardtack biscuits, a waterskin, and a crowbar and hammer.

One of the most important items in your dungeoneering pack is a set of wooden torches. Set one on fire, and you'll have a light to see by, helping you navigate traps and search for treasure. Of course, torches might also give away your location if anyone else happens to be watching.

EXPLORER'S PACK

Waterskin

Bedroll

Cup

Square Tin

Rations

Tinderbox

Any adventurer may be called upon to endure a long journey while fulfilling a quest, but those who have chosen the life of an explorer are especially well prepared for travel.

An explorer's pack includes a backpack, a bedroll, torches, a tinderbox, a waterskin, and some rope, plus a mess kit for preparing and eating food, which usually includes a square tin, a cup, and cutlery. The pack will also include several days' worth of rations.

VAMPIRE HUNTER'S PACK

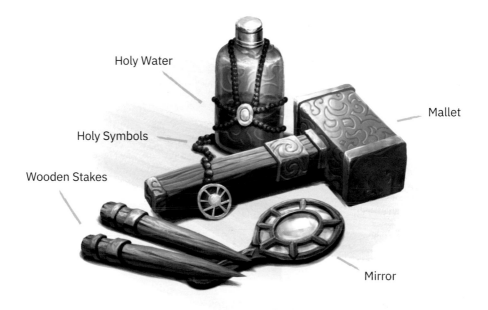

Holy Water

Holy Symbols

Wooden Stakes

Mallet

Mirror

Vampires are incredibly dangerous creatures with a frightening array of occult abilities, and experienced vampire hunters may spend years developing the perfect set of tools to fight these monsters.

Of course, even an apprentice vampire hunter will be given the essentials, usually in a beautifully crafted wooden chest. These include wooden stakes and a mallet, which is used to drive a stake into a vampire's heart, plus a mirror to help detect the fiends, and holy water and holy symbols, sacred to their own particular god, to chase the wretches away.

USING HEROES
TO TELL YOUR OWN STORIES

Growling sounds and the scrape of steel against steel echoed around the broken statues and other debris in the chamber. Six goblins wielding notched spears and rusty swords moved toward Whey-Shu from all sides.

The kenku monk waited. She was not the type to make the first move in battle. The dark feathers all over her body quivered slightly from the movement of the air, but she was otherwise absolutely still. It was better to size up her opponents and look for flaws in their combat technique than to recklessly charge forth into close combat too soon.

The largest of the goblins, clearly the pack leader, spoke with a snarl.

"Surrender, little bird, or we'll clip your wings."

Whey-Shu knew that even if she did give up, they would never let her leave this place alive. She also knew that goblins were impulsive creatures. If they were hesitating instead of charging immediately at her, then it must be because they knew who she was and feared what she was capable of.

Perhaps this would be a worthy challenge after all. . . .

Reading about adventure is a great way to stir your imagination, and creating a character is an important first step in composing your personal stories. Building a new character is about discovering who they are at the beginning of their journey and then figuring out who they might become as their legend grows across the land.

Your idea might start with a single hero or a small group of adventurers, but it can go *anywhere*: a creature's lair, the village nearby, cities and dungeons, caverns or skyscapes. You get to choose all the ingredients and stir them together. To help you as you develop your story, here are some questions to keep in mind:

WHO ARE YOUR CHARACTERS?

- Are your heroes like you or different? Young or old, human or something else? Think about the foes you must face. Great heroes require great challenges. What makes your villains memorable and powerful, and what brings them into conflict with your adventurers?

WHERE DOES YOUR STORY TAKE PLACE?

- At the top of a mountain, in a serene forest, deep underwater, or in a creepy boneyard?

WHEN DOES THE STORY HAPPEN?

- At night or during the day, in the middle of a thunderstorm or right before the bells toll to ring in the new year? Think about time passing as your story unfolds.

HOW DO THINGS CHANGE AS THE STORY PROCEEDS?

- Do your heroes succeed or fail? Do they find somewhere new or explore someplace old?

WHAT SHOULD SOMEONE FEEL AS THEY EXPERIENCE YOUR STORY?

- Do you want them to laugh or get scared? Cheer or be grossed out?

WHY ARE YOUR HEROES GOING ON THIS ADVENTURE?

- Knowing what their goals are will help you create a compelling tale of courage and exploration.

Remember, you don't have to answer all these questions by yourself! DUNGEONS & DRAGONS is a collaborative game where you work with your friends to create your own stories. One person acts as a narrator, called a Dungeon Master, and the other players each take on the role of a hero, called a Player Character, in the adventuring party in a story. The Dungeon Master sets up a scene by describing a place and any threats that may exist, and then each player contributes ideas by explaining their own character's actions. With each scene created by the group, the story moves forward in unexpected and entertaining ways.

If you don't feel confident starting from scratch, you can go to your local gaming store and play a DUNGEONS & DRAGONS demonstration session. Demos can be a quick way to learn how the game is played and an opportunity to possibly make some brand-new friends at the same time.

After you've read through all the character options in this little heroic handbook, there's even more DUNGEONS & DRAGONS material to ignite your imagination. The *Monsters & Creatures* guide is bursting at the seams with beasts and critters for you and your friends to discover. You know who your hero is and have equipped them for their journey, now find our what dangers lurk in the darkness and *answer the call to adventure!*

Published in the United States by Ten Speed Press, an imprint of Random House, a division of Penguin Random House LLC, New York.
www.crownpublishing.com
www.tenspeed.com

Ten Speed Press and the Ten Speed Press colophon are registered trademarks of Penguin Random House LLC.

Library of Congress Cataloging-in-Publication Data
Names: Zub, Jim, author. | Conceptopolis, illustrator.
Title: Warriors & weapons : a young adventurer's guide : Dungeons & dragons /
    written by Jim Zub ; illustrations by Conceptopolis.
Other titles: Warriors and weapons
Description: First Edition. | New York : Ten Speed Press, an imprint of the
    Crown Publishing Group, [2019] | Audience: Grades 4 to 6. | Audience:
    Ages: 8-12. | Includes index.
Identifiers: LCCN 2018050293| ISBN 9781984856425 (Hardcover) |
    ISBN 9781984856432 (eBook)
Subjects: LCSH: Dungeons and dragons (Game)—Handbooks, manuals,
    etc.—Juvenile literature. | Dungeons and dragons (Game)—Pictorial
    works—Juvenile literature.
Classification: LCC GV1469.62.D84 Z837 2019 | DDC 793.93—dc23
LC record available at https://lccn.loc.gov/2018050293

Hardcover ISBN: 978-1-9848-5642-5
eBook ISBN: 978-1-9848-5643-2

Printed in China

Publisher: Aaron Wehner
Art Director and Designer: Betsy Stromberg
Editors: Patrick Barb and Julie Bennett
Managing Editor: Doug Ogan
Production Designer: Lisa Bieser
Wizards of the Coast Team: David Gershman, Kate Irwin, Adam Lee, Hilary Ross, Liz Schuh
Illustrations: Conceptopolis, LLC

10 9 8 7 6 5 4 3 2 1

First Edition